THE CHRISTIAN TE
GENERAL ROB

Copyright © 2003 Edward R. DeVries
ISBN: 978-1-387-095553-7

Published by:
Dixie Heritage Press
www.dixieheritage.net

TABLE OF CONTENTS

Foreword (by Dr. Larry Lilly)..5

Author's Introduction..7

Part One - The Christian Testimony of Robert E. Lee as Evidenced by his:

Chapter One: Early Life and Student Record..........................9

Chapter Two: Relationship with his Family............................11

Chapter Three: Faithfulness to Religious Service...................13

Chapter Four: Tenure as President of Washington College........17

Chapter Five: Efforts to Seek the Conversion of Souls..............21

Chapter Six: Expressed Joy Over the Conversion of Souls.........23

Chapter Seven: Prayer Life...25

Chapter Eight: High Esteem of the King James Bible...............27

Chapter Nine: The Way He Lived the Scripture......................29

Chapter Ten: A Man without Vice.......................................37

Chapter Eleven: Conscience, Duty, and Financial Integrity.........39

Chapter Twelve: Prayerful Decision to Join Confederacy...........41

Chapter Thirteen: Restraint and Compassion in Combat...........43

TABLE OF CONTENTS - *Continued*

***Part Two - The Christian Testimony of
Robert E. Lee is Evidenced by:***

Chapter Fourteen: Other's Comments About his Faith............45

Chapter Fifteen: The Eulogies Given in his Memory................47

***Part Three - The Christian Testimony of
Robert E. Lee as Evidenced by the:***

Chapter Sixteen: Personal Testimony of General Lee..............53

Part Four -

Chapter Seventeen: Conclusion......................................55

Appendixes -

Appendix One: Misc. Quotes About Robert E. Lee….….........57

Appendix Two: Meet General Lee in Heaven...........….……...67

End Notes...71

FOREWORD
By Dr. Larry Lilly
Editor of Braveheart Magazine

The Christian Testimony of General Robert E. Lee is a must read for anyone interested in General Lee, the Christian faith, or the building of character. You may search the entirety of Christian history and be hard pressed to find a better example of faithfulness and virtue. When looking up the definition of "Integrity" in a dictionary I wouldn't be surprised to be instructed to, "See Robert E. Lee." Friends and enemies alike attest to his gigantic character.

Dr. Edward R. DeVries has performed a service to all people of faith who aspire in times of severe testing to rise above petty humanness and be true to Christ and heavenly ideals. He has searched and researched the bulk of extant literature on General Lee. The sources listed in the endnotes, if read, would qualify the reader as an expert on the life and heritage of Robert E. Lee.

Dr. DeVries has not attempted to deify the General. Rather, he has used his wordsmith power to paint a cameo of rare beauty paying tribute to one of Americas grandest Gentlemen.

Larry Lilly

February 19, 2003

AUTHOR'S INTRODUCTION

I begin my book <u>A Symbol of Hate? or an Ensign of the Christian Faith?: The Truth About the Confederate Battle Flag</u>, by telling the story of my life journey from "died in the wool" Yankee to Southern Patriot. So I was not always an admirer of Robert E. Lee. In fact, throughout my childhood and well into my adult years I considered him, and all southern men of his era, to be traitors. For the life of me I couldn't figure out why General Grant didn't just shoot them all at Appomattox.

Having been born in Hammond, Indiana, the closest I had ever come to "Southern Culture" was having been raised on the SOUTH SIDE of Chicago. I was educated in "Yankee" schools to believe that the North rightly won the "Civil War." I grew up believing that Abraham Lincoln was a great president and Jefferson Davis was a traitor. I also grew up believing that Ulysses S. Grant was a hero and Robert E. Lee was not.

During my Sophomore year at Hyles-Anderson College (an Indiana school) I was called to a ministry position in Texas. But still, I managed to maintain my Yankee pride for several years while living in Texas.

Then having been asked to teach a college level course on American History I decided that I had better "brush up" on the "Civil War." It was during this study that, to my shock and surprise, I came to the conclusion that **the South was Right**.

About 18 months later, I invited my good friend, Dr. Roy Branson (a preacher from Tennessee), to come and preach a revival in the church I was pastoring. The interesting thing about Dr. Branson is that he can never make it through a sermon without drawing an illustration from the life of General Douglas MacArthur. However, during one of his sermons he didn't make his usual observation from the life of the great WWII General. Instead, he commented on the Christian character of Confederate General Robert E. Lee.

"So Lee was a Christian?" – I said to myself. The next week I began to research the life of General Lee. I was so impressed with what I read about the life of Lee that I quickly found that he was becoming one of my heroes. So much so that shortly after Dr. Branson left I obtained a portrait of the General which is the first thing a visitor will see when he comes into my office. Through the years since that revival meeting I have read 37 biographies of General Lee, including the 707 page <u>Memoirs of Robert E. Lee</u>.

Some of those 37 biographies were written by admirers of Lee. Others were written by men who wanted only to criticize him. But in every biography, regardless of whether or not it was written by friend or foe, two things stood out:

1- His Christian Character. Even his critics were forced to admit that Robert E. Lee was a man of sincere Christian faith. Even his critics were forced to admit that there was no immorality or religious hypocrisy in the life of Lee.

2- His admirers wrote of his virtues and, because his life, letters, and speeches were totally free of vice, malice, or impropriety of any kind his critics had nothing to criticize him for except those same virtues. It speaks highly of a man when he is criticized for virtue. While many critics said he was "too religious" or a "religious fanatic" – none of his critics called him a hypocrite or accused him of any impropriety. One critic said the General was, "too great a gentleman and that is why he lost the war."[1] That may be true but I could hardly look down upon a man for being a "gentleman." I also fail to see how any man could be "too great a gentleman."

So while none of the 37 biographers had set out to write a book about the Christian testimony and religious character of General Robert E. Lee, his character and faith were strongly evident in all 37 biographies.

So I have set out to write such a book. Would to God that the project had been undertaken by a better writer than myself. May the Lord Jesus Christ be glorified in the retelling of Lee's life, as I know He was glorified in the General's life.

Edward R. DeVries
John 3:30

CHAPTER ONE

GENERAL LEE'S CHRISTIAN TESTIMONY IS EVIDENCED IN HIS EARLY LIFE AND STUDENT RECORD

Like most children in the South of his era, Robert E. Lee was home-schooled during his early years. Beginning at the age of six his mother began young Robert's formal instruction in the "Three R's" (Reading, wRiting, and aRithmatic). Additionally, she instructed him in Music, Literature, and Scripture. Biographer William J. Johnson describes Mrs. Lee as a:

> ...devoted mother, gentle and pious, with a sincere and simple faith in God's providence. She appears to have been a woman of high character, and to have taught her son practical as well as moral excellence.[2]

In <u>Anecdotes and Letters of General Robert E. Lee</u> we read that his mother:

> ...watched over his daily life and "planted him in the soil of truth, morality, and religion, so that his boyhood was marked by everything that produces nobility of character in manhood."[3]

British General Viscount Wolseley writes:

> It was from her lips he learned the Bible, from her teaching he drank in the sincere belief in revealed religion which he never lost. It was she who imbued her great son with an ineradicable belief in the efficacy of prayer, and in the reality of God's interposition in the everyday affairs of the true believer.[4]

As a teenager, Lee was enrolled in the Alexandria Academy where he was a model student. Unlike the typical adolescents of any era, it was said of Lee that,

> No breach of discipline nor any neglect of duty was ever charged against him during his years of study in Alexandria Academy.[5]

After finishing his high school studies at Alexandria Academy, Lee enrolled in a preparatory school administered by Benjamin Hallowell, a Quaker, who was for many years a famous teacher in Alexandria. He says Lee:

> ...was a most exemplary student in every respect. He was never behind time at his studies; never failed at a single recitation; was perfectly observant of the rules and regulations of the institution; was gentlemanly, unobtrusive, and respectful in all his deportment to teachers and his fellow students.[6]

When Lee entered West Point in 1825, then Superintendent, Colonel Thayer, wrote in his official report to President John Quincy Adams, that, "drunkenness and dissipation" were "generally prevalent among the young men."[7] Yet in the midst of this moral depravity it was said of Cadet Lee that:

> He never drank intoxicating liquor, never used tobacco, or indulged in any of the petty vices to which youth are apt."[7]

While a student at West Point he never received a reprimand, mark, or demerit.[8] General A. L. Long's biography of Lee summarizes his student record by saying:

> Throughout his whole student life he performed no act which his pious mother could not have fully approved.[9]

General Lee was a Christian who, with the encouragement of his mother, began to live his religion at a very young age. Christian character demonstrated in irreproachable conduct set young Robert E. Lee apart from the rest of his classmates at the Alexandria Academy, during his preparatory school years, and at West Point. The same character and conduct would be maintained throughout the whole of Lee's life, causing him, in all stations of life, to rise to the top of whatever group he was in.

CHAPTER TWO

GENERAL LEE'S CHRISTIAN TESTIMONY CAN BE SEEN IN HIS RELATIONSHIP WITH HIS FAMILY

General Long's biography of Lee says that, "As a son his attachment to his mother knew no bounds. His affection for his wife was, if possible, even stronger."[10] Of Lee's affection toward their seven children Long says he was, "exceedingly fond of his family"[11] As both a biographer, and as one who served in close quarters with Lee throughout the war, General Long was amazed at, "how little of war and how much of Christian feeling and domestic affection his home letters contain."[12] On page 397, Long writes:

> Nor was his attention solely given to the cares of camp and field. His warm affection for his wife and children never for a moment ceased, and his letters to them breathe the spirit of the quiet father of a family, not of the great warrior engaged in deadly fray. Seldom has a general busied in the details of a mighty war written home a letter so full of wise fatherly counsel and deep affection.[13]

Captain J. William Jones says, "These family letters shown that a happier home circle could not be found than that of this loving family."[14]

CHAPTER THREE

GENERAL LEE'S CHRISTIAN TESTIMONY CAN BE SEEN IN HIS FAITHFULNESS TO RELIGIOUS SERVICES

AS A BOY

As a boy Lee, "worshipped in old Christ Church, Alexandria, Virginia, in the same church in which Washington had been a pewholder."[15]

AS A YOUNG OFFICER IN THE ARMY

"The summer months of 1860 were spent in San Antonio. While there Lee interested himself with the good people of that town in building an Episcopal church, to which he contributed largely."[16]

DURING THE WAR

In his book Joy in the Camp, author Charles Jennings writes:

> With ... the moral support of President Jefferson Davis and General Robert E. Lee, many pastors and evangelists would hold religious services in the camps while the army was idle between campaigns, immediately before many battles and even during the heat of battle itself.[17]

Of these wartime services General Long writes,

> General Lee took great pleasure in this display of religious emotion. He gave it every encouragement, conversed with the chaplains, and assisted them in their labors to the utmost of his power. He requested their prayers for himself, and exhibited that sincere religious faith which was ever a strong element in his character.[18]

Regarding Lee's attendance of these meetings, Chaplain J. Wilbur Jones commented,

> That reverent worshiper who kneels in the dust during prayer, or listens with sharpened attention and moist eyes as the preacher delivers his message, is our beloved commander-in-chief, General R. E. Lee.[19]

During the winter months of 1864-65 when General Lee and his 30,000 remaining troops were holding their line against General Grant's overwhelming numbers, the soldiers and officers of Lee's army built 60 chapels at his command. It was reported that sometimes one could stand in one spot and hear two or three religious meetings going on at the same time.[20]

In addition to attending all of the religious services in the field, General Lee made every effort to attend Sunday morning services in a local church. In his personal notebook General Long writes,

> When encamped near Richmond, General Lee would ride into the city on Traveler before breakfast for early Sunday morning service . . . then ride back to camp for breakfast.[21]

AFTER THE WAR

In the latter part of June 1865, General Lee and his family moved to a small cottage in the country, near Cartersville, Virginia. There he spent several months of quite and rest. Captain Edmund Randolph Cocke wrote that,

> During that summer he was a regular attendant at the various churches in our neighborhood, whenever there was a service.[22]

William Johnson gives this account:

> Robert E. Lee and his family attended Saint Paul's Episcopal Church in Richmond.
>
> Among the memorial windows in the church are two to General Robert E. Lee . . . One of them represents Moses leaving Pharaoh's court to join his lot with his own oppressed people,

with the scriptural text bearing thereon – "By faith Moses refused to be called the son of Pharaoh's daughter, choosing rather to suffer affliction with the children of God, as seeing Him who is invisible."[23]

DURING HIS YEARS AT WASHINGTON COLLEGE

Dr. J. William Jones says,

> He was a most regular attendant upon all of the services of his own church, his seat in the college chapel was never vacant... and if there was a union prayer meeting, or a service of general interest in any of the churches of Lexington, General Lee was sure to be among the most devout attendants.[24]

"Upon these chapel devotions General Lee was an unfailing attendant, and his religious sincerity had a marked influence upon all about him."[25]

LEE WAS NOT ONLY A FAITHFUL ATTENDER BUT ALSO AN ENTHUSIASTIC PARTICIPANT

"His pew in his own church was immediately in front of the chancel, his seat in the chapel was the second from the pulpit; he seemed always to prefer a seat near the preacher's stand. He always devoutly knelt during prayer, and his attitude during the entire service was that of an interested listener or a reverential participant."[26]

"He never failed to attend preaching... Nor was he a mere listless attendant. The simple truths of the Gospel had no more attentive listener than General Lee; and his eyes would kindle and his face glow under the more tender doctrines of grace. He used frequently to attend preaching at Jackson's headquarters; and it was a scene which a master-hand might have delighted to paint – those two great warriors, surrounded by hundreds of officers and men, bowed in humble worship before the God and Saviour in whom they trusted."[27]

"General Lee was a most active promoter of the interests of his church, and of the cause of Christ in the community; and all of the pastors felt that they had in him a warm friend."[28]

"He was a most liberal contributor to his church and to other objects of benevolence."[29]

In fact, the general's last public act was a motion that he made in a church business meeting to raise the pastor's salary. When the elders and congregation complained that the church lacked the funds to provide the increase the general personally pledged the funds.[30]

CHAPTER FOUR

GENERAL LEE'S CHRISTIAN TESTIMONY CAN BE SEEN IN HIS TENURE AS PRESIDENT OF WASHINGTON COLLEGE

During the War, the United States Army confiscated General and Mrs. Lee's home at Arlington (now Arlington National Cemetery) along with most of his family's wealth. At war's end the General and his family were homeless, penniless, and in debt. So at a stage in life when most men would look forward to settling into a well-earned retirement, Lee began looking for a job. He was offered several high-paying positions including the presidency of an insurance company in Nashville, salary, $10,000 per year. The position Lee chose instead was that of the presidency of a small Christian college in Virginia.

Washington College was so named because its financial endowment had come from the nation's first president. The college had seen its share of wartime activity, having lost most of her buildings to enemy fire, and the enrollment had dropped, according to various reports, to somewhere between twenty and sixty students. The school, like Lee, was practically bankrupt and the trustees, while setting General Lee's salary at a mere $1,500 per year, had no way of guaranteeing that the college could pay. So Lee, seeing an opportunity to mold young men for Christ, accepted the position as a faith ministry, trusting that the Lord would provide for his salary and needs.

> On Monday October 2, 1865, "after solemn and appropriate prayer by the Rev. W. S. White, D.D., the oldest Christian minister in the town," Lee was ordained president of Washington College. His salary was to be fifteen hundred dollars – "offered purely on a basis of faith!"[31]

Dr. J. William Jones writes that:

> The college expand[ed] under his magic touch, until, from an institution with five professors and some sixty students, it numbered more than twenty instructors and over four hundred students.[32]

General Lee

> ...became personally acquainted with each student, and so accurate was his remembrance of their names that...He won the confidence of students... The students honored and loved the president, and sedulously avoided transgressions that would cause him pain.[33]

General Lee's Memoirs record that:

> Upon matriculation of a new student his religious faith was inquired into, and it was sought at once to bring him into close relations with the pastor.[34]

Lee's first act, as President of the college, called for the

> ...erection as soon as possible of a chapel, which should be of dimensions suitable for the demands of the college. There were other objects calling for a greater outlay of money than the resources of the college afforded, but he deemed this of great importance, and succeeded in getting appropriations for it before undertaking any other projects. He hastened the selection of the site and the drawing of the plans. The completion of the work was much retarded owing to the want of funds, "but his interest in its erection never flagged. He gave his personal superintendence from first to last, visiting it often two or three times a day." This building is now known as the Lee Memorial Chapel.[35]

After it was dedicated in 1867 he always attended morning prayers and all other exercises held there. His son Robert said:

> Whenever I was there on a visit, I went with him every morning to chapel. He had a certain seat which he occupied, and you could have kept your watch regulated by the time he entered the doors. As he thought well of the young men who left his drawing room by ten o'clock, so he placed in a higher estimate those who attended chapel regularly, especially if they got there in proper time.[36]

Writing in 1907, Professor Edward Joynes of the University of South Carolina described Lee's philosophy of education thusly:

> He thought it to be the office of a college not merely to educate

the intellect, but to make Christian men. The moral and religious character of the students was even more precious in his eyes than their intellectual progress and was made the special object of his constant personal solicitude. In his annual reports to the trustees, which were models of clear and dignified composition, he always dealt with particular emphasis upon these interests, and nothing in the college gratified him more than its marked moral and religious improvement during his administration.[37]

After his death, during the memorial service held at the First Presbyterian Church of Nashville, General Lee was quoted to have said:

> I shall be disappointed sir; I shall fail in the leading object that brought me here, unless these young men all become Christians.[38]

J. William Jones quoted Lee as saying:

> I dread the thought of any student going away from the college without becoming a sincere Christian.[39]

CHAPTER FIVE

GENERAL LEE'S CHRISTIAN TESTIMONY CAN BE SEEN IN HIS EFFORTS TO SEEK THE CONVERSION OF OTHERS

On page 117 of the 1912 textbook <u>Lee the American</u> we read:

> A devout Christian himself, he thought of every soldier in his army as a soul to be saved, and in every way he could, encouraged the mission and revival work which went on all through the war with ever-increasing activity. Even in the midst of urgent duty he would stop and take part in a camp prayer meeting and listen to the exhortations of some ragged veteran, as a young convert might listen to an apostle.[40]

Page 242 of the same textbook says:

> So concerned was Lee for the spiritual welfare of his soldiers that one of his biographers says, "One almost feels as if he cared more for winning souls than battles, and for supplying his army with Bibles than with bullets."[41]

On page 51 of the book, <u>Christ in the Camp</u> we read:

> General Lee always took the deepest interest in the work of his chaplains and the spiritual welfare of his men. He was a frequent visitor at the chaplains' meetings, and a deeply interested observer of their proceedings; and the faithful chaplain who stuck to his post and did his duty could be always assured of a warm friend at headquarters.[42]

His personal witnessing to the troops, his tireless efforts on behalf of the chaplains, and his orders promoting religious activity in the camps of the Confederate Army were used of God to bring a revival in the Army of Northern Virginia that, according to historian Charles A. Jennings, resulted in the conversion of over 50,000 souls.[43]

CHAPTER SIX

GENERAL LEE'S CHRISTIAN TESTIMONY CAN BE SEEN IN HIS JOY OVER THE CONVERSION OF SOULS

Chaplain Jones gave the following account of one of his meetings with General Lee:

> ...as we presently began to answer his questions concerning the spiritual interests of the army, and to tell of the great revival which was then extending through the camps and bringing thousands of our noble men to Christ, we saw his eye brighten and his whole countenance glow with pleasure; and as, in his simple, feeling words, he expressed his delight, we forgot the great warrior and only remembered that we were communing with an humble, earnest Christian.[44]

In 1865, after the war ended, a general revival of religion extended throughout the State of Virginia. A former army chaplain told General Lee about it, and said that "large numbers of the returned soldiers were among the converts." Upon hearing this news, General Lee began to cry, and replied, "I am delighted to hear that; I wish that all of them would become Christians."[45]

During the great revival which followed in the Virginia Military Institute, also located in Lexington, in 1869, in which 110 cadets professed conversion, he said to his pastor, with deep emotion: "I rejoice to hear that. It is the best news I have heard since I have been in Lexington. Would that we could have such a revival in all our colleges!"[46]

CHAPTER SEVEN

GENERAL LEE'S CHRISTIAN TESTIMONY CAN BE SEEN IN HIS PRAYER LIFE

A 1900 article in *The Chautauquan* described General Lee as, "…a man of prayer, he had his regular hours of secret devotion which he allowed nothing else, however pressing, to interrupt."[47]

"General Lee always had his family alter and read family prayers every morning just before breakfast. A daughter-in-law, after her first visit to General Lee, spending three weeks there, said that she did not believe he would have an entirely high opinion of any person, even General Washington, if he could return to earth, if he were not in time for family prayers."[48]

General Lee's son was quoted as saying, "family prayers were read every morning just before breakfast."[49]

During the war, General Lee issued many orders in the field calling his troops to prayer. Here is an example of such an order:

> Knowing that intercessory prayer is our mightiest weapon and the supreme call for all Christians today, I pleadingly urge our people everywhere to pray. Believing that prayer is the greatest contribution that our people can make in this critical hour, I humbly urge that we take time to pray - to really pray.
>
> Let there be prayer at sunup, at noonday, at sundown, at midnight - all through the day. Let us pray for our children, our youth, our aged, our pastors, our homes. Let us pray for our churches.
>
> Let us pray for ourselves that we may not lose the word "concern" out of our Christian vocabulary. Let us pray for our nation. Let us pray for those who have never known Jesus Christ and redeeming love, for moral forces everywhere, for our national leaders.
>
> Let prayer be our passion. Let prayer be our practice.[50]

CHAPTER EIGHT

GENERAL LEE'S CHRISTIAN TESTIMONY CAN BE SEEN IN HIS ESTEEM OF THE KING JAMES BIBLE

General Lee's two favorite books, which he always kept in his small private library, and which were, "in constant use," were the "Episcopal Prayer Book and the Bible."[51]

Biographer William J. Johnson writes:

> The Bible was his daily companion, his guide, his comfort, and his trust. He was a constant reader, and a diligent student of God's Word, and had his regular seasons for this delightful exercise. In the army he read his Bible every day, in his headquarters, on the march, or in bivouac; and he did everything in his power to circulate the Word of God among his soldiers.[52]

Chaplain Jones described the pocket Bible which Lee carried with him throughout the war as "well used."[53] Jones went on to write that, "…he had marked many passages, especially those teaching the great doctrines"[54]

In a letter to a group of European admirers, Lee wrote the following in a letter dated Monday, April 16, 1866, in which he refers to the Bible as:

> …a book in comparison with which all others in my eyes are of minor importance; and which in all my perplexities and distresses has never failed to give me light and strength.[55]

"There are things in the old Book which I may not be able to explain, but I fully accept it as the infallible Word of God, and receive its teachings as inspired by the Holy Spirit."
-- General Robert E. Lee[56]

General Lee described the Bible as, "a book which supplies the place of all others, and one that cannot be replaced by any other."[57]

Dabney Carr Harrison heard Lee say, "The virtue and fidelity which should characterize a soldier, can be learned from the holy pages of the Bible alone."[58]

"During the war he was an active promoter of Bible distribution among his soldiers, and soon after coming to Lexington he accepted the presidency of Rockbridge Bible Society, and continued to discharge its duties up to the time of his death."[59]

CHAPTER NINE

GENERAL LEE'S CHRISTIAN TESTIMONY CAN BE SEEN IN THE WAY HE LIVED THE SCRIPTURE

To Lee, the Bible was not just a book to be read and admired, it was The Book upon which he based his life and conversation.

General Lee's "life verse" was Psalm 37:31, "The law of his God is in his heart; none of his steps shall slide."[60]

Below is an incomplete listing of some of the verses that General Lee had underscored in his Bible with accompanying examples of how he applied the passages in his daily life.

- **Ecclesiastes 9:10, "*Whatsoever thy hand findeth to do, do it with thy might.*"**

As a student at West Point, Lee was so attentive to his studies that he graduated at the head of his class.[61]

- **Proverbs 5:18, "*rejoice with the wife of thy youth.*" vs. 19, let her, "*satisfy thee at all times; and be thou ravished always with her love.*"**

"His wife had become a confirmed invalid, and to her he gave devoted attention. He spent much of his leisure time in her company, cheering her spirits by his conversation while he wheeled her invalid chair about."[62]

- **Proverbs 15:4, "A wholesome tongue is a tree of life: but perverseness therein is a breach in the spirit."**

Mr. James Eveleth, who was a clerk in the Engineer Department at Fortress Monroe, while Lieutenant Robert E. Lee was stationed there from 1829-1834 said:

> There never was a man more universally loved and respected. He never uttered a word among his most intimate associates that might not have been spoken in the presence of the most refined woman. It can always be said of him that he was never heard to speak disparagingly of anyone, and where anyone was heard so to speak in his presence, he would always recall some trait of excellence in the absent one.[63]

- **Proverbs 21:23,** *"Whoso keepeth his mouth and his tongue keepeth his soul from troubles."*

General Long quotes an elder in one of the churches where Lee attended but where he was never a member as saying:

> ...his lips were never soiled by a profane or obscene word, and that when the provocation was great for a display of angry feelings it was his course to use "the soft answer which turneth away wrath."[64]

- **James 1: 26,** *"If any man among you seem to be religious, and bridleth not his tongue, but deceiveth his own heart, this man's religion is vain."*

"His most intimate friends never heard him utter an oath."[65]

"One who knew him from his boyhood to his grave declared that he never knew him 'to utter an immoral or profane word. He never used slang nor told a joke which his wife and daughters might not have listened to with perfect propriety.'"[66]

- **I Timothy 5:1 & 17, "Rebuke not an elder... Let the elders... be counted worthy of double honour, especially they who labour in the word and doctrine."**

"Lee was not accustomed to indulge in carping criticisms of sermons"[67]

- **Matthew 5:44, "Love your enemies, bless them that curse you, do good to them that hate you, and pray for them which despitefully use you, and persecute you."**

Chaplain J. William Jones said, "No man, living or dead, ever heard General Lee utter an unkind word to a prisoner, or saw him maltreat in the slightest degree, any who fell into his power."[68]

- **Proverbs 18:24, "A man that hath friends must show himself friendly:"**

"His son, Captain Robert E. Lee, Jr., tells of hearing two ladies who were visiting Lee say, 'Everybody and everything – his family, his friends, his horse, his dog – loves Colonel Lee."[69]

- **Acts 10:34 says that, "God is no respecter of persons."**

And neither was General Lee: "…in his treatment of his subordinates. He had no favorites, no unworthy partialities."[70]

- **Proverbs 25:21, "If thine enemy be hungry, give him bread to eat; and if he be thirsty, give him water to drink."**

Dr. J. William Jones relates the following:

> One day in the autumn of 1869, I saw General Lee standing at his gate, talking to a humbly clad man, who turned off, evidently delighted with his interview, just as I came up. After exchanging salutations, the General pleasantly said, pointing to the retreating form, 'That is one of our old soldiers who is in necessitous circumstances.' I took it for granted that it was some Confederate, and asked to what command he belonged, when the General quietly and pleasantly added, 'He fought on the other side, but we must not remember that against him now.'

The man afterward came to my house and said to me, in speaking of his interview with General Lee: 'Sir, he is the noblest man that ever lived. He not only had a kind word for an old soldier who fought against him, but he gave me some money to help me on my way.'

What a beautiful illustration of the teaching of the Apostle: 'If thine enemy hunger, feed him; if he thirst, give him drink'!"[71]

- **Psalm 128:2,** *"For thou shalt eat the labour of thine hands: happy shalt thou be, and it shall be well with thee."*

Soon after he went to Lexington [1865], he was visited by an executive of a certain insurance company, who offered him their presidency, at a salary of $10,000 a year. He told the agent that he was compelled by the Lord to serve as President of Washington College and feared that the time required to manage an insurance company would, without doubt, require him to neglect his duties as president of Washington College.

"But, General," said the executive, "we do not want you to discharge any duties. We simply want the use of your name; that will abundantly compensate us."

"Excuse me, sir," was the prompt and decided rejoinder; "I cannot consent to receive pay for services I do not render."[72]

- **Proverbs 22:1,** *"A good name is rather to be chosen than great riches."*

In further reply to the above incident General Lee told the insurance executive:

> My good name is about all that I have saved from the wreck of the war, and that is not for sale.[73]

HE WAS NEVER BITTER

"General Lee uttered no word of personal bitterness toward the people of the North. He referred to them as 'those people' or as 'our friends across the river.' During the war 'he did not for a single moment forget that he led the army of a people who professed to be governed by the principles of Christian civilization, and that no outrages on the part of others could justify him in departing from these high principles.'"[74]

General Lee was often quoted to have said:

> I have fought against the people of the North because I believed they were seeking to wrest from the South dearest rights. But I have never cherished toward them bitter or vindictive feelings, and have never seen the day that I did not pray for them.[75]

"It is related that one day during the war, as they were reconnoitering the countless hosts opposed to them, one of his subordinates exclaimed in bitter tones, 'I wish those people were all dead!' General Lee, with that inimitable grace of manner peculiar to him, promptly rejoined: 'How can you say so General? Now I wish that they were all at home attending to their own business and leaving us to do the same.'"[76]

CONSIDERATE OF OTHERS

"Lee always manifested the liveliest interest in the welfare of his men, and was deeply touched by their hardships and privations. Being invited upon one occasion to dine at a house where an elegant dinner was served, it is related that he declined all of the rich viands offered him, dined on bread and beef, and quietly said to the lady of the house, 'I cannot consent to be feasting while my poor soldiers are nearly starving.'"[77]

"When General Lee's intention of writing his military history became known, it excited the liveliest interest among military instructors and commandants of military establishments in foreign countries…The project, as conceived by General Lee, had not been to rear a memorial to his military genius, but to vindicate and set forth the valor of his soldiers."[78]

"Well Colonel [Thomas H.] Carter, if I turn those men out of their rooms, where will they sleep?" "on the ground?" "I replied at once, 'Like the rest of the army.'"   "None of your blarney, Colonel Carter – none of your blarney, sir' he replied with a smile."[79]

"No commander was ever more careful of his men, and never had care for the comfort of an army given rise to greater devotion. He was constantly calling to the attention of the authorities the wants of his soldiers, and making every effort to provide them with food and clothing. The feeling for him was one of love, not of awe or dread. They could approach him with the assurance that they would be received with kindness and consideration, and that any just complaint would receive proper attention. There was no condescension in his manner, but he was ever simple, kind, and sympathetic, and his men, while having unbounded faith in him as a leader, almost worshipped him as a man. These relations of affection and mutual trust between the army and its commander had much to do with the undaunted bravery displayed by the men, and bore a due share in the victory they gained."[80]

The following is told by a Union Veteran:

> I had been a most bitter anti-South man, and fought and cursed the Confederates desperately. I could see nothing good in any of them. The last day of the fight I was badly wounded. A ball shattered my leg. I lay on the ground not far from Cemetery Ridge, and as General Lee ordered retreat, he and his officers rode near me.
>
> As they came along I recognized him, and though faint from exposure and loss of blood, I raised my hands, and looked Lee in the face, and shouted as loud as I could – 'Hurrah for the Union!'
>
> The General heard me, looked, stopped his horse, dismounted, and came toward me. I confess I at first thought he meant to kill me. But, as he came up, he looked down at me with such a sad expression on his face that all fear left me, and I wondered what he was about. He extended his hand to me, grasping mine firmly, and looking right into my eyes said: "My son, I hope you will soon be well."

If I live a thousand years, I shall never forget the expression on General Lee's face. There he was, defeated, retiring from a field that had cost him and his cause almost their last hope, and yet he stopped to say words like these to a wounded soldier of the opposition who had taunted him as he passed by![81]

HE ALWAYS ASSUMED RESPONSIBILITY

"As he judged of the work of others, so he judged his own."[82]

"He...assumed the responsibility of the failure of movements which a less strong and generous spirit would have made his subordinates bear."[83]

This is illustrated in a conversation that took place in his last meeting with his staff before the surrender to General Grant at Appomattox:

> "Oh, general, what will history say of the surrender of the Army in the field?" "Yes, I know they will say hard things of us: they will not understand how we were overwhelmed with numbers. But that is not the question colonel: the question is, Is it right to surrender this army? If it is right, then I will take **all** the responsibility."[84]

General Lee was, "...far above any petty jealousy."[85]

HE WAS ALWAYS GRATEFUL

Dr. T.V. Moore tells how General Lee never failed to acknowledge a kindness:

> During the summer of 1864 I had occasion to render him a slight service, so slight that, knowing at the time that he was sick and overburdened with responsibilities of his position, I never expected it to be acknowledged at all; but, to my surprise, I received a letter thanking me for this trivial service, and adding: "I thank you especially that I have a place in your prayers. No human power can avail us without the blessing of

God, and I rejoice to know that in the crisis of our affairs, good men everywhere are supplicating Him for His favor and protection."[86]

AND HE ALWAYS HELD HIS TEMPER

"Colonel A. L. Long, his military secretary, speaks of 'General Lee's losing his temper – a circumstance which happened only twice, to my knowledge, during my long acquaintance with him. He was not wanting in temper, but was on the contrary, a man of decided character and strong passions; yet he had such complete control of himself that few men ever knew him to deviate from his habitual calm dignity.'"[87]

One of only 2 times Lee lost his temper:

> General Lee could hear from his tent something of this conversation, but caught from it only that Goode was talking of matters that scouts, as a rule, were permitted to tell only to the commanding general himself. So, coming to the door of his tent, he called out with a stern voice that he did not wish his scouts to talk in camp. He spoke very angrily, and stepped back into his tent. Goode fairly trembled. The aide-de-camp, however, went forward to the General's tent and told him that the scout, who was devoted to Stuart and naturally very anxious for his safety, was only endeavoring to mark accurately on the map the point at which the diversion of the artillery fire was to be made, and was by no means talking from the mere desire to talk. General Lee came out at once from his tent, commanded his orderly to have supper with hot coffee put on the table for Goode, made him sit in his own camp-chair at the table, stood at the fire near by, and performed all the duties of a hospitable host to the fine fellow. Few generals ever made such thorough amends to a private soldier for an injustice done him in anger.[88]

CHAPTER TEN

GENERAL LEE'S CHRISTIAN TESTIMONY CAN BE SEEN IN THAT HE WAS A MAN WITHOUT VICE

General Long, in his biography of Lee, recalls an incident when, in a private conversation, a gentleman once said to an officer who had been intimately associated with General Lee:

> "Most men have their weak point. What was General Lee's?" After a thoughtful pause the answer was, "I really do not know."[89]

On the same page of this biography, Long says that General Lee was:

> ...singularly free from the faults which so often mar the character of great men. He was without envy, jealousy, or suspicion, self-seeking, or covetousness; there was nothing about him to diminish or chill the respect which all men felt for him.[90]

A near relative wrote after his death"

> I knew Robert Lee from the time I can first remember, and I never recollect, and I never remember hearing him censured for anything in my life.[91]

In recounting his first meeting with General Lee, Confederate Vice-President Alexander H. Stephens, commented:

> I had preconceived ideas of the rough soldier with no time for the graces of life, and by companionship almost compelled to the vices of his profession. I did not know then that he used no stimulants, was free even from the use of tobacco, and that he was absolutely stainless in his private life. I did not know then, as I do now, that he had been a model youth and young man; but I had before me the most manly and entire gentleman that I ever saw.[92]

Many biographers note the fact that in his entire life General Lee never used tobacco, never drank an intoxicating beverage, and never used profane language.[93] In regard to his character and total lack of vice, British general Viscount Wolseley started his famous 1906 biography of Lee by saying:

> I desire to make known to the reader not only the renowned soldier, whom I believe to have been the greatest of his age, but to give some insight into the character of one whom I have always considered the most perfect man I ever met.[94]

CHAPTER ELEVEN

GENERAL LEE'S CHRISTIAN TESTIMONY CAN BE SEEN IN HIS BEING A MAN OF CONSCIENCE, DUTY, AND FINANCIAL INTEGRITY

☐ CONSCIENCE

General Pendleton summed up General Lee's character by saying:

> What his conscience dictated and his judgment decided, there his heart was.[95]

There was no hesitation or vacillation about him:

> When he had once formed a plan the orders for its execution were positive, decisive, and final.[96]

General Grant interpreted him correctly when he said:

> I knew there was no use to urge him to anything against his ideas of right.[97]

☐ DUTY

His closest aide, General Long, said,

> In his life he exhibited an ambition not for self, but for the discharge of what he conscientiously deemed his duty; and no allurements or emoluments of place or profit could seduce him from his firmly fixed convictions.[98]

His son Robert was quoted as saying: "His idea of life was to do his duty, at whatever cost, and to try to help others do theirs."[99]

In fact, General Lee only accepted the offer to command the armies of the newly formed Confederacy because he believed it to be his duty to his native land of Virginia. He committed himself to this duty with a full appreciation of the risk involved.

General Pendleton recalls the following interview with Lee:

> I have never believed we could, against the gigantic combination for our subjugation, make good in the long run our independence unless foreign powers should, directly or indirectly, assist us...But such consideration made with me no difference. We had, I was satisfied, sacred principles to maintain and rights to defend, for which we were in duty bound to do our best, even if we perished in the endeavor.[100]

☐FINANCIAL INTEGRITY

"At the close of the war, offers of financial assistance poured upon him from all quarters – houses, lands, and money; but he steadfastly refused them. An English nobleman, thinking that he would rejoice in some place of retreat, wrote to offer him a splendid country seat in England and an annuity of $15,000. His reply was simple and noble: 'I am deeply grateful, but I cannot consent to desert my native state in the hour of her adversity. I must abide her fortunes and share her fate.'"[101]

CHAPTER TWELVE

GENERAL LEE'S CHRISTIAN TESTIMONY CAN BE SEEN IN HIS PRAYERFUL DECISION TO JOIN THE CONFEDERATE ARMY

We discussed in the last chapter that General Lee, joined the Confederate Army because he believed it was his duty to do so. The decision was also made as the result of earnest and intense prayer.

When United States president Abraham Lincoln realized that the secession of the Southern States was a reality, he immediately began preparing for war. If the Southern States could not be quickly talked into rejoining the Union he would invade the Southern States and bring them back into the Union at the point of guns. To do this, President Lincoln needed to raise an army. And the man he chose to command that Army was Colonel Robert E. Lee.

Colonel Lee was brought to Washington and offered a promotion (ahead of dozens of "senior" officers) to the rank of Full General and Supreme Commander of the Armies of the United States.

At the same time, Colonel Lee was also offered command of the Army of Virginia.

So Colonel Lee had a choice. Accept promotion in the Federal Army to the rank of Full General or resign his Federal commission and accept Command of the Virginian Army?

He knew that the Federal Army out-manned and out-gunned the Confederate Army. He also knew that the Northern Government had more money than the Southern Government, and that the Northern States had a greater capacity to produce the materials of war than did the Southern States. Ultimately, as evidenced by the quote in the last chapter, he realized that the Northern States could win the war in their own right while the Southern States could only win in the unlikely event that some foreign power chose to intervene on their behalf.

Colonel Lee committed this decision, as he did most others, to prayer. Mrs. Lee gave the following account of how his decision was made:

> The night his letter of resignation was to be written, he asked to be left alone for a time, and while he paced the chamber above, and was heard frequently to fall upon his knees and engage in prayer for divine guidance [she] waited and watched and prayed below.
>
> At last he came down, early in the morning of April 20, 1861, calm, collected, almost cheerful, and said: "well Mary the question is settled. Here is my letter of resignation and a letter that I have written to General Scott."[102]

His wife's words to him were:

> Whichever way you go will be in the path of duty. You will think it right and I shall be satisfied.[103]

His decision to resign his commission in the Federal Army and to turn down Lincoln's offer to command the Armies of the United States having been settled by prayer, he made his decision to accept the command of the Army of Virginia while attending services on Sunday morning, April 21, 1861, at Christ Church in Alexandria, Virginia. Lee announced that after, "counting the agonizing cost to his state," he, "agreed to take command of the Virginia forces."[104]

It was in this same church, on a Sunday morning 87 years previous, that George Washington announced his decision to, 'fight to uphold the independence of the colonies.'"[105]

CHAPTER THIRTEEN

GENERAL LEE'S CHRISTIAN TESTIMONY CAN BE SEEN IN HIS RESTRAINT AND COMPASSION AS A MILITARY COMMANDER

As Rush Limbaugh often says on his radio show, "the purpose of war is to kill people and break things." While both actions are unavoidable in the execution of war, neither of them are war's true purpose. Sadly, throughout history, it seems that few commanders realized this. Most of history's generals fought their wars according to the Rush Limbaugh philosophy. According to this thinking, whoever kills the most people and destroys the most property wins – even if they fail to bring about or prevent the political objectives over which the war was originally declared.

But to every rule there are exceptions. And General Lee was definitely one of those rare exceptions. As Commanding General of the Army of Northern Virginia and of the Confederate Armies, Lee made sure that his men knew and followed the "rules of war." He went out of his way to determine that any prospective action would effect the desired political or military advantage before he undertook it. Then, if he determined that death and destruction were necessary, he engaged in such activity only to the degree that it was necessary to achieve the necessary end – and he made sure that his targets were only those of a military nature. He never attacked or victimized civilians, not even in enemy territory.

General Lee's Christian philosophy of war can best be illustrated in the order that he gave his men before their invasion of the Northern state of Pennsylvania. It is his famous GENERAL ORDER #73:

> The duties exacted of us by civilization and Christianity are not less obligatory in the country of the enemy than in our own. The commanding general considers that no greater disgrace could befall the army, and through it our whole people, than the perpetration of the barbarous outrages upon the innocent

and defenseless and the wanton destruction of private property that have marked the course of the enemy in our own country.

It must be remembered that we make war only on armed men, and that we cannot take vengeance for the wrongs our people have suffered without lowering ourselves in the eyes of all whose abhorrence has been excited by the atrocities of our enemy, and offending against Him to whom vengeance belongeth, without whose favor and support our efforts must all prove in vain.

The commanding general, therefore earnestly exhorts the troops to abstain with most scrupulous care from unnecessary or wanton injury to private property, and he enjoins upon all officers to arrest and bring to summary punishment all who shall in any way offend against the orders on this subject.

R. E. Lee
General

In regard to Lee's execution and his men's observance of the above order, General Gordon noted that:

> …even in his triumphant entry into the territory of the enemy, so regardful was he of civilized warfare that the observance of his general order as to private property and private rights left the line of his march marked and marred by no devastated fields, charred ruins, or desolated homes.[106]

General Lee conducted all of his business in a Christian-like way, even the business of war. Historian Charles Jennings writes:

> When Lee and his army were in enemy territory, he insisted that his men fight and survive according to the laws of fairness, justice and integrity. In spite of the fact that many Union officers were known for their brutality against southern civilians, Lee forbade "unnecessary or wanton injury to private property" and made it mandatory that his men pay for all food, forage, and supplies that they acquired from northern farmers and merchants.[107]

CHAPTER FOURTEEN

GENERAL LEE'S CHRISTIAN TESTIMONY CAN BE SEEN IN THE ASSESSMENTS OF OTHERS REGARDING HIS FAITH

- **Historian Charles Jennings, from his book, <u>A Character Sketch of Robert E. Lee</u>[108]:**

"Among the Many Outstanding Qualities of Lee's Character, His Christian Faith was Paramount!"

"...humble Christian servant of the South."

"[A] man of sterling Christian character"

- **Historian William J. Johnson, from his <u>Biography of Robert E. Lee</u>[109]:**

"Not a chaplain in his army excelled him in personal piety or in devoutness."

"Those who knew General Lee in private could not fail to remark that religion was with him something more than an empty name; that it was a power lodged in the heart and controlling his whole nature."

- **Author James C. Young:**

"Alexander believed in himself, Caesar in his legions, Napoleon in his destiny, Lee in his God"[110]

- **Federal General Montgomery C. Meigs said:**

"He was a model of a soldier and the beau-ideal of a Christian."[11]

45

- **Faculty Members of Washington College:**

"...he was a model of an elevated Christian and an upright gentleman."[112]

"That Lee's Christian character was highly regarded in England is evidenced by the fact that several English admirers sent him a handsome copy of the Bible, through the Honorable A. W. Beresford Hope. The dedication reads: 'General Robert E. Lee, Commanding the Confederate Army, from the undersigned Englishmen and Englishwomen, recognizing the Genius of the General, admiring the Humanity of the Man, respecting the Virtues of the Christian.'"[113]

"The religious phase of Lee's character may be summed up in three short sentences: He trusted and loved God. He loved his fellow men. He believed in Jesus Christ as his Saviour and Lord, and manifested the Christian spirit toward enemies as well as friends."[114]

CHAPTER FIFTEEN

GENERAL LEE'S CHRISTIAN TESTIMONY CAN BE SEEN IN THE EULOGIES SPOKEN AFTER HIS DEATH

General Long's biography states that:

> The death of General Lee was solemnly proclaimed to the residents of Lexington by the tolling of bells. With common accord all business was suspended. Tokens of mourning appeared on all buildings. The schools were closed and the college exercises ceased.
>
> The grief manifested by the people was profound. The little children whom he had cherished, and who had entertained for him a reverential role, wept over the absence of one whose death they scarce understood. Women were affected to tears, and strong men turned aside to suppress their emotion. It was a personal loss to them.
>
> In the Southern States his death was deplored as a calamity. Citizens, societies, and all associations of men met in some manner of assemblage and recorded their sense of the sad event. Resolutions of condolence and respect were adopted. Legislatures paused in their proceedings to add to the tokens of grief. All professions, all callings in mercantile life, were represented in tributes.
>
> Rarely has sorrow been so universal, and seldom has genuine affection entered so deeply over the death of a public benefactor.[115]

In addition to the main services, held on the campus of Washington College in Lexington, memorial services were held in practically every city, town, and village of the South; and also in several Northern States. The following eulogies, final tributes to the unwavering Christian faith of the beloved General, were given at various memorial services and/or printed in various newspapers, throughout the nation.

Rev. R.A. Holland gave the following eulogy in a memorial address at the Kentucky Military Institute:

> Behold in him a character which, if not perfect, conceals its faults with the effulgence of its virtues, even as the sun conceals the spots on its dazzling disk.[116]

The following eulogy appeared in the *Southern Collegian*, the student paper of Washington College:

> He died as he lived, calmly and quite, in the full assurance of the Christian's faith, and with the brightest evidence that, in "passing over the river," he has, with his great Lieutenant Stonewall Jackson, "rested under the shade of the trees" of paradise."[117]

Dr. T. V. Moore, delivering a eulogy during the memorial service in Nashville summed up Lee's "unselfish nobleness" as follows:

> Other men have been great warriors, yet only great in success. It was his to show his uttermost greatness in failure. Other men had conquered victory; it was his sublime preeminence to conquer defeat, and transform it into the grandest triumph. Other warriors have betrayed ambition, cruelty, and avarice in success, weakness, littleness, and selfishness in disaster; but he developed the unselfish nobleness of his nature when, bowing submissively to the resistless decrees of Providence, he sheathed his unsullied blade; and refusing the most tempting offers to engage in commercial and monetary enterprises; refusing the gifts that a grateful though impoverished people longed to lavish on him; refusing every attempt to bring him where public applause would so heartily have greeted him – he retired to the cloistered shades of his chosen position, without a word of repining, and consecrated himself to the youth of his country, not to breath into them a spirit of vindictive hate; not to train them for political struggles only, but to lead them to Jesus, and make them noble citizens, by making them sincere Christians.[118]

The following eulogy was written by the editor of the *New York Herald*:

> He was beloved by slaves for his kindness and consideration

toward them...Noted for his piety...a regular attendant at church.

Having perfect command of his temper, he was never seen angry, and his most intimate friends never heard him utter an oath. Indeed it is doubtful if there are many men of the present generation who unite so many virtues and so few vices in each of themselves as did General Lee.

He came nearer the ideal of a soldier and Christian general than any man we can think of, for he was a greater soldier than Havelock, and equally as devout a Christian.[119]

Charles A. Dana, Lincoln's Assistant Secretary of War, wrote the following eulogy for the *New York Sun*:

> Whatever may be the verdict as to his career in public life, the universal expression will be that in General Lee an able soldier, a sincere Christian, and an honest man has been taken from earth.[120]

Senator Benjamin Hill gave the following eulogy in a memorial address:

> He was a foe without hate, a friend without treachery, a soldier without cruelty, and a victim without murmuring. He was a public officer without vices, a private citizen without wrong, a neighbor without reproach, a Christian without hypocrisy, and a man without guile. He was Caesar without his ambition, Frederick without his tyranny, Napoleon without his selfishness, and Washington without his reward. He was as obedient to authority as a servant and royal in authority as a king. He was as gentle as a woman in life, pure and modest as a virgin in thought, watchful as a Roman vestal, submissive to law as Socrates, and grand in battle as Achilles.[121]

Confederate States President, Jefferson Davis, gave the following eulogy:

> Robert E. Lee was my associate and friend in the Military Academy, and we were friends until the hour of his death. We were associates and friends when he was a soldier and I was a congressman, and associates and friends when he led the armies of the Confederacy and I held a civil office, and therefore I may claim to speak as one who knew him.

> In the many sad scenes and perilous circumstances through which we passed together our conferences were frequent and full, yet never was there an occasion on which there was not entire harmony of purpose and accordance as to means. If ever there was a difference of opinion, it was dissipated by discussion, and harmony was the result.
>
> ...I never in my life saw in him the slightest tendency to self-seeking. It was not his to make a record, it was not his to shift blame to other shoulders, but it was his, with an eye fixed upon the welfare of his country, never faltering, to follow the line of duty to the end. His was the heart that braved every difficulty: his was the mind that wrought victory out of defeat.[122]

General Lee's compassion and Christian conduct, even in war, is evidenced in this eulogy by General John B. Gordon:

> General Lee is known to the world only as a military man, but it is easy to divine from his history how mindful of all just authority, how observant of all constitutional restrictions, would have been his career as a civilian.
>
> When, near the conclusion of the war, darkness was thickening about the falling fortunes of the Confederacy, when its very life was in the Sword of Lee, it was my proud privilege to note with special admiration the modest demeanor, the manly decorum, and the respectful homage which marked all his intercourse with the constituted authorities of his country. Clothed with all power, he hid its every symbol behind a genial modesty, and refused to exert it save in obedience to law.
>
> And even in his triumphant entry into the territory of the enemy, so regardful was he of civilized warfare that the observance of his general order as to private property and private rights left the line of his march marked and marred by no devastated fields, charred ruins, or desolated homes.[123]

General Long gives the following eulogy in his biography of Lee:

> ...his memory will pass down the ages as representing all that is greatest in military art, as well as what is truest, bravest, and noblest in human life – a soldier who never failed in duty, a man who feared and trusted God and served his generation."[124]

Even the Canadian newspapers commented on the faith of General Lee. The following is from a eulogy that appeared in the *Halifax Morning Chronicle*:

> He was gentle and just... Above all he was faithful.
>
> There was no man in his own ranks or that of the enemy that doubted his faith.[125]

CHAPTER SIXTEEN

GENERAL LEE'S CHRISTIAN TESTIMONY CAN BE SEEN IN HIS PERSONAL TESTIMONY

General Lee once told Chaplain Jones that he was just, "a sinner saved by grace... cleansed in the atoning blood of Christ." He concluded by saying that his, "only hope of salvation was built on the Rock of Ages."[126]

Southern Partisan magazine quoted General Lee as saying:

> I can only say that I am nothing but a poor sinner trusting in Christ alone for salvation.[127]

Once, when asked what was his life's goal, Lee replied:

> My chief concern is to try to be an humble, earnest Christian.[128]

A thorough searching of public databases failed to uncover a modern day political or military leader making equally unashamed and fundamental statements of faith.

CHAPTER SEVENTEEN

CONCLUSION

In his popular seminars on "corporate leadership" Dr. John C. Maxwell often quotes Abraham Lincoln and or draws from incidents in his life to illustrate various "leadership principles." Maxwell is an outspoken critic of the Southern Confederacy. So it surprised me when in his *21 Irrefutable Laws of Leadership* seminar Maxwell, after having spoken for hours on the "virtues of Lincoln" and applying them to leadership, said that he was forced to admit that the nation's greatest example of a leader was not Abraham Lincoln but General Robert E. Lee.

Maxwell told how in 1861 President Lincoln offered command of the Armies of the United States to then Colonel Lee. Maxwell then told how all of the ranks of the Army were fixed on Colonel Lee, waiting to see what side he would take in the arising conflict. Then, when Lee had made his decision to decline Mr. Lincoln's offer and command the Southern Army many of the officers of the United States Army resigned their commission to serve under Lee. Many of the men who resigned to serve under Lee's command had actually outranked him in the Federal Army. Many of them hailed from the North. Maxwell says that Lee made no effort to recruit from the ranks of Lincoln's Army. He asked none to resign their commissions and leave with him. Yet when he had made his decision the brightest and most capable officers of the Federal Army all followed his course of action. They all considered it an honor to serve under him. Maxwell concluded by saying that the ranks of the officer corps followed Lee because Lee, in his life, exhibited all of the qualities of leadership. Maxwell said that Lee lived in such a way that people just naturally followed him. His conclusion was that if you want people to follow you, then you must be a man of "**character**."[129]

Douglas Southall Freeman likewise distilled Robert E. Lee's visible life into one word -- "Character!"[130]

I submit in this final chapter that the source of General Lee's character was Christ.

In his classic book <u>An Imitation of Christ</u>, Saint Thomas Aquinas states that one lives the Christian by imitating Christ in his daily life. The most devout Christian being of course the one who best imitates Christ.

But Paul the Apostle taught just the opposite. In **Galatians 2:20** he writes, ***"I am crucified with Christ: nevertheless I live; yet not I, but Christ liveth in me."*** Or in other words, The Christian life is not lived as we imitate Christ, but rather, the Christian life is lived as we YIELD (Romans 6:13 and 16) ourselves to Christ and allow HIM to live His life THROUGH us.

The degree in which we as believers yield ourselves to Christ determines the degree to which Christ can live through us. Therefore the greatest Christians are those who are the most surrendered to Christ their Lord.

And the character for which General Lee is known serves as evidence that Lee was surrendered to his Lord in every area of life.

At the risk of seeming redundant, General Lee was a great man because he was a great Christian. He was a great Christian because he was totally surrendered to the Lord Jesus Christ and because Christ was so completely able to live through him.

So while the temptation in writing a book such as this would be to conclude by encouraging the reader to imitate the actions and character of General Lee, I must rather conclude by admonishing the reader to surrender wholly to Jesus Christ so that Christ might live through us as He did so many years ago through Lee. May the retelling of General Lee's life ever bring us to our knees and into our Bibles. May the Lord Jesus Christ be glorified in our lives as He was through the life of General Robert E. Lee.

If you do not know Jesus Christ as your Lord and Saviour I pray that you will turn immediately to **APPENDIX TWO – Will You Meet General Lee in Heaven?**. In it, you will find the first key to living a life surrendered to Christ.

APPENDIX ONE

The first time I read a biography about someone I generally find myself looking for more information on the man, his life, his work, etc. Since, for some readers, this may be their first biography of General Lee, and since I have limited the chapters of this book to one specific aspect of his life, his Christian Testimony, some readers may find themselves wanting to learn more about the man and his life than what has been provided in the previous pages. To this end, I provide the following quotes.

While reading various biographies and reference works about General Lee I have extracted numerous quotes about the man, his character, incidents in his life, etc. Many of them are contained throughout the body of the book. Others that were not used in the body of the book are supplied below:

- **MODEL YOUTH AND YOUNG MAN**

"...we are assured that Lee's childhood was as remarkable as his manhood for the modesty and thoughtfulness of his character and for the performance of every duty which devolved upon him.'"[131]

- **MILITARY CAREER**

"...he was made a captain in 1838"[132]

"...in 1848 he was made a colonel."[132]

"In 1849, Lee moved to Baltimore, Maryland, where he lived three years."[132]

"Lee was appointed superintendent of West Point Military Academy in 1852 and remained there three years."[132]

"In 1855 he was made a Lieutenant Colonel in the regular army and entered upon his new duties. In 1855-57 he was stationed in Texas."[132]

"...he was selected by the Secretary of War to suppress the famous 'John Brown Raid' and was sent to Harper's Ferry in Command of the United States troops. Brown was captured and handed over to the proper civil authorities. Afterward Lee remarked to Mrs. Pickett's father, 'I'm glad we didn't have to kill him, for I believe he is an honest, conscientious old man.'"[133]

"In February 1860 Lee was commanded to take command of the Department of Texas."[134]

"In June, 1865, the United States Grand Jury in Norfolk, Virginia, indicted General Lee and others for treason."[134]

- **RESIGNATION FROM UNITED STATES ARMY**

On Thursday, April 18, 1861 Lee was offered command of the Armies of the United States. Lee's Reply to President Lincoln was: "I look upon secession as anarchy... but how can I draw my sword upon Virginia, my native State?"[135]

"Lee then told Army Chief of Staff General Scott that he, '...could take no part in the invasion of the Southern States.'"[136]

Lee's Letter of Resignation read as follows:

> I therefore tender my resignation, which I request you will recommend for acceptance. It would have been presented at once but for the struggle it has cost me to separate myself from a service to which I have devoted the best years of my life and all the ability I possessed.
>
> Save in the defense of my native state I desire never again to draw my sword.[137]

When asked years later if he had any regrets, Lee said to General Wade Hampton, in July, 1869:

> I could have taken no other course save in dishonor; and if it were to be gone over again, I should act in precisely the same way.[138]

- **PHILOSOPHY OF WARFARE**

"I think our policy should be purely on the defensive – to resist aggression and allow time to allay the passions and permit reason to resume her sway."[139]

- **COMMAND OBSTACLES**

The following is from General Long's biography:

> Grant's rank as commander-in-chief of the Federal armies enabled him to wield them all in concert for the great aim which he had in view. . . General Lee possessed no such comprehensive authority. He was commander of a single army only, and while his advice in relation to the movements of other armies was constantly asked by the Government, it was not always followed.
>
> The commander-in-chief was eventually given him, it is true, but too late for it to be more than an empty honor. Had he had from the beginning of his contest with Grant possessed authoritative control of all military resources of the Confederacy, the management of the war would certainly have been more efficient, and the armies of the Gulf States must have been handled with better judgment and success than they were under the orders of the civil authorities. The power of resistance of the Confederacy would probably have been protracted, and it is within the limits of possibility that eventual success in the effort to gain independence might have been attained, though at the late stage of the war this had become almost hopeless.[140]

- **HIS OPINION OF NEWSPAPER GENERALS**

His opinion of newspaper generals, those talented editors who have no difficulty in wielding armies and winning victories from editorial rooms, was satirically expressed in a conversation with the Hon. B. H. Hill ...

> We made a great mistake, Mr. Hill, in the beginning of our struggle ... we appointed all our worst generals to command the armies, and all our best generals to edit the newspapers.

As you know I have planned some campaigns and quite a number of battles. I have given the work all the care and thought I could, and sometimes, when my plans were completed, as far as I could see they seemed perfect. But when I have fought them through I have discovered defects, and occasionally wondered I did not see some of the defects in advance. When it was all over I found by reading the newspaper that these best editor-generals saw all the defects plainly from the start. Unfortunately they did not communicate their knowledge to me until it was too late... I have no ambition but to serve the Confederacy and do all I can to win our independence. I am willing to serve in any capacity to which the authorities assign me. I have done the best I could in the field, and have not succeeded as I should wish. I am willing to yield my place to these best generals and I will do my best for the cause in editing a newspaper.[141]

- **MILITARY GENIUS:**

During the Mexican War, General Scott was heard to declare: Lee is the Greatest Military genius in America.[142]

Years later General Scott said: Robert Lee would be worth fifty thousand men.[143]

General Preston, at memorial service, tells of a conversation he had with General Scott, in which Scott said:

> I tell you if I were on my deathbed tomorrow, and the President of the United States should tell me that a great battle was to be fought for the liberty or slavery of the country, and he asked my judgment as to the ability of a commander, I would say with my dying breath, "Let it be Robert E. Lee."[144]

The Cuban Junta in New York ask him to, "lead their revolutionary movement on the island."[145]

- **ABILITY TO CONFOUND THE ENEMY**

At Appomattox, on the afternoon of the day of the surrender, Federal General Meade, made a visit to Lee at his headquarters. In the course of their conversation he remarked:

> Now that the war may be considered over, I hope that you will not deem it improper for me to ask, for my personal information, the strength of your army during the operations at Richmond and Petersburg?

General Lee replied:

> At no time did my force exceed 35,000 men; often it was less.

With a look of surprise Meade answered:

> General, you amaze me! We always estimated your force at about 70,000 men.

During the interview Lee turned to Meade, who had been associated with him as an officer in the "old army" and said:

> Meade, years are telling on you: your hair is getting quite gray.

Meade's reply:

> Ah, General Lee, it is not the work of years: you are responsible for my gray hairs.[146]

- **PERSONAL MODESTY**

While many generals headquartered in the area's finest homes General Lee:

> ...rarely slept in a house – never outside his lines – during the war, and when on the march some convenient fence-corner would be his most frequent place of bivouac. The writer has not infrequently seen some colonel, or major-quartermaster, entertained in princely style at some hospitable mansion, while nearby the commander-in-chief would bivouac in the open air.
>
> He never allowed his mess to draw from the commissary more than they were entitled to, and not infrequently he would sit down to a dinner meager in quality and scant in quantity.[147]

Immediately after the war when riding from Appomattox to Richmond:

61

His soldierly habits remained unchanged. At one house where he stopped for the night he declined the comfortable bed that had been prepared for him, but slept upon his blanket which he had spread upon the floor. Stopping at the house of his brother, Charles Carter Lee, in Powhatan, he spent the evening in conversation, but at bedtime, despite the fact that rain was falling, he took up his quarters in his well worn tent.[148]

In November, 1863, the City Council of Richmond passed a resolution to purchase for Lee an elegant mansion, as a small token of the high esteem in which he was held by the city which he had so long defended.

> Arlington was in the hands of the United States government, the "White House" on York River [the house of George Washington's early wedded life] had been ruthlessly burned by Federal soldiers, his splendid estate had nearly all passed from his control, and his salary in Confederate scrip was utterly inadequate to support in a proper style his invalid wife and accomplished daughters. These facts were known to the city authorities, and they but reflected the popular wish in the action that they took.
>
> But when General Lee heard of it, he wrote as follows to the president of the Council:
>
>> I assure you sir, that no want of appreciation of the honor conferred upon me by this resolution, or the insensibility to the kind feelings which prompted it, induces me to ask, as I most respectfully do, that no further proceedings be taken with reference to the subject. The house is not necessary to the use of my family, and my own duties will prevent any residence in Richmond.
>>
>> I should therefore be compelled to decline the generous offer, and I trust that whatever means the City Council may have to spare for this purpose may be devoted to the relief of the families of our soldiers in the field, who are more in want of assistance, and more deserving of it, than myself.[149]

- **WELL REGARDED BY OTHERS**

One night some soldiers were overheard discussing the tenets of Atheism around their camp fire, when a rough, honest fellow cut short the discussion by saying: "Well, boys, the rest of us may have developed from monkeys; but I tell you none less than a God could have made a man as Marse Robert!"[150]

Charles Cornwallis Chesney, distinguished British military critic said of Lee: "In strategy mighty, in battle terrible, in adversity as in prosperity a hero indeed, with the simple devotion to duty and the rare purity of a Christian knight, he joined all the kingly qualities of a leader of men.[151]

General Wilcox later said: "All who knew him were prepared to accept him at once as a general when he was assigned to the command of the Army of Northern Virginia, and his success, great as it was, was only what had been anticipated."[152]

Just before Appomattox:

> The remnant of that noble army, now reduced to 10,000 effective men, was marshaled to cut its way through a host of 75,000 strong; but, notwithstanding the stupendous odds, there was not in that little band a heart that quailed or a hand that trembled; there was not one of them who would not willingly have laid down his life in the cause they had so long maintained, and for the noble chief who had so often led them to victory.[153]

General Hunt at Appomattox: "This was the last time I saw General Lee – a truly great man, as great in adversity as in prosperity.[154]

The following was recorded of his post-war ride to Richmond:

> Shortly after the surrender General Lee returned to Richmond...everywhere on his road to Richmond he received tokens of admiration and respect from both friend and foe.
>
> On reaching Richmond the party passed sadly through ... a distressing scene of blackened ruins. He was quickly recognized and the inhabitants flocked out in multitudes to meet him, cheering and waiving hats and handkerchiefs.
>
> General Lee, to whom this ovation could not have been agreeable, simply raised his hat in reply to the greetings of the citizens, and rode to his house on Franklin Street. The closing of its doors on his retiring form was the final scene in that long

drama of war in which he had for years been the central figure. He had returned to that private family life for which his soul had yearned even in the most active years of the war, and had become once more, what he had always desired to be, a peaceful citizen of a peaceful land.[155]

He was the:

>...confidant and advisor of a great number of the young men belonging to the best class of Virginia families. To him they were constantly writing for information, assistance, encouragement, and advice, and upon his opinion they based their own action.[156]

- **FAMOUS LAST WORDS**

"Strike the tent!"[157]

- **HIS DISDAIN FOR DRUNKENESS**

"During the war he was accustomed to do everything in his power, both by precept and example, to prevent drunkenness among his officers and men, and more than once he refused to promote an officer who drank too freely, saying, 'I cannot consent to place in control of others one who cannot control himself.'"[158]

- **MOST PRIZED WORLDLY POSSESSION**

"He then took up another sword, plain and dull in appearance as compared with the other. This he showed with great pride. It was the sword presented to General Washington during the Revolutionary War...this he kept with him during our war."[159]

- **FAVORITE BEVERAGE**

"...buttermilk."[160]

- **DEPRAVATIONS OF WAR**

October 20, 1862, Daughter Annie dies.[161]

1862, granddaughter dies.[161]

"About this time came the death of his daughter-in-law, whose husband, major-general W. H. F. Lee, was kept a prisoner at Fortress Monroe for nine, long, weary months."[161]

General Lee was thus described toward the end of the war:

> He had aged somewhat in appearance since the beginning of the war, but had rather gained than lost physical vigor from the severe life he had led. His hair had grown gray, but his face had the ruddy hue of health and his eyes were as clear and bright as ever. His dress was always a plain gray uniform, with cavalry boots reaching nearly to his knees, and a broad-brimmed gray felt hat. He seldom wore a weapon, and his only marks of rank were the stars on his collar. Though always abstemious in diet, he seemed able to bear any amount of fatigue, being capable of remaining in his saddle all day and at his desk half the night.[162]

APPENDIX TWO

WILL YOU MEET GENERAL LEE IN HEAVEN?

My friend, I am asking you the most important question of your life. Your joy or your sorrow for all eternity depends upon your answer. The question is: Are you saved? It is not a question of how good you are, nor if you are a church member, but are you saved? Are you sure you will go to Heaven when you die?

God says in order to go to Heaven, you must be born again. In John 3:7, Jesus said to Nicodemus, *"Ye must be born again."*

In the Bible, God gives us the plan of how to be born again, which means to be saved. His plan is simple! You can be saved today. But how?

First, my friend, you must realize that you are a sinner. *"For all have sinned, and come short of the glory of God." (Romans 3:23)*

Because you are a sinner, you are condemned to die: *"For the wages [payment] of sin is death." (Romans 6:23).* This includes eternal separation from God, in Hell.

Further, *"it is appointed unto men once to die, but after this the judgment." (Hebrews 9:27)*

But God loved you so much that he gave his only begotten Son, Jesus, to bear your sin and die in your place: *"For he hat made him [Jesus, who knew no sin] to be sin for us...that we might be made the righteousness of God in him." (II Corinthians 5:21)*

Jesus had to shed his blood and die. *"For the life of the flesh is in the blood" (Leviticus 17:11).* Further, *"without shedding of blood is no remission." (Hebrews 9:22)*

"But God commendeth his love towards us, in that, while we were yet sinners, Christ died for us." (Romans 5:8) Although we cannot understand how, God said my sins and your sins were laid upon Jesus, and he died in our place. He became our substitute. It is true; God cannot lie.

My friend, *"God...now commandeth all men every where to repent" (Acts 17:30)*

This repentence is a change of mind that agrees with God that one is a sinner, and also agrees with what Jesus did for us on the cross.

In Acts 16:30-31, the Philippian jailer asked Paul and Silas *"Sirs, what must I do to be saved?* and they said, *Believe on the Lord Jesus Christ, and thou shalt be saved."*

Simply believe on him as the one who bore your sin, died in your place, was buried, and whom God resurrected.

His resurrection powerfully assures that the believer can claim everlasting life when Jesus is received as Saviour.

"But as many as received him, to them gave he power to become the sons of God, even to them that believe on his name." (John 1:12)

"For whosoever shall call upon the name of the Lord shall be saved." (Romans 10:13)

"Whosoever" includes you! *"Shall be"* means not *maybe*, nor *can*, but *"shall"* be saved.

Surely, you realize that you are a sinner. Right now, wherever you are, repenting, lift your heart to God in prayer.

In Luke 18:13, a sinner prayed *"God be merciful to me a sinner."* Just pray: "Oh, God, I know I am a sinner. I believe that Jesus was my substitute when he died on the cross. I believe his shed blood, death, burial, and resurrection were for me. I now receive him as my Saviour. I thank you for the forgiveness of my sins, the gift of salvation and everlasting life, because of your merciful grace. Amen."

Just take God at his word and claim his salvation by faith. Believe, and you will be saved. No church, no lodge, no good works can save you. Remember, God does the saving. All of it!

God's simple plan of salvation is: You are a sinner. Therefore, unless you believe on Jesus who died in your place, you will spend eternity in Hell. If you believe on him as your crucified, buried, and risen Saviour, you receive forgiveness for all of your sins and his gift of eternal salvation by faith.

You say, "Surely, it cannot be that simple!" Yes, that simple. It is scriptural; it is God's plan. My friend, believe on Jesus and receive him as Saviour today.

If his plan is not perfectly clear, read this appendix over and over, without laying it down until you understand it. Your soul is worth more than all the world.

"For what shall it profit a man, if he shall gain the whole world, and lose his own soul?" (Mark 8:36)

Be sure you are saved. If you lose your soul, you miss Heaven and lose all. Please! Let God save you this very moment.

God's power will save you, keep you saved, and enable you to live a victorious Christian life. *"There hath not temptation taken you but that such as is common to man: but God is faithful, who will not suffer you to be tempted above that ye are able; but will with the temptation also make a way to escape, that ye may be able to bear it." (I Corinthians 10:13)* Do not trust your feelings; they change. Stand on God's promises; they *never* change. After you are saved, there are three things to practice daily for spiritual growth: Pray; you talk to God. Read your Bible; God talks to you. Witness; you talk for God.

You should be baptized in obedience to the Lord Jesus Christ, as a public testimony of your salvation, and then unite with a Bible-believing church without delay. *"Be not therefore ashamed of the testimony of our Lord." (II Timothy 1:8)*

"Whosoever therefore shall confess me before men, him will I confess also before my Father which is in heaven." (Matthew 10:32)

Additional Helpful Verses		
John 3:16	I Peter 2:24	Isaiah 53:6
James 1:15	Romans 10:9-10	Ephesians 2:8-9
Proverbs 27:1	I Corinthians 15:3-4	John 10:27-31
	I John 5:13	

If you have received Christ as your Saviour as a result of reading this, I would like to hear from you and send you a free booklet that will help you to grow as a Christian. I will also do my best to put you in contact with a friendly Bible-preaching church in your area. Please write to me and let me know of your decision today! **Dr.DeVries@bibleschool.edu**

END NOTES

1 - *The Believer's Banner*, Pastor John Stephen Brown, Bainbridge, Indiana
2 - *Biography of Robert E. Lee*, William J. Johnson, Christian Liberty Press
3 - *Anecdotes and Letters of General Robert E. Lee*, Dr. J. William Jones, 1875, D. Appleton & Co., pg. 21
4 - *General Lee* by Viscount Wolseley, George P. Humphrey Co., 1906, pg. 13
5 - *Biography of Robert E. Lee*, William J. Johnson, Christian Liberty Press
6 - *The Life of Robert E. Lee*, General A.L. Long 1887 J.M. Stoddard & Co. pg. 27
7 - *Popular Life of General Robert E. Lee*, Emily V. Mason, 1874, J. Murphy & Company, pg.26
8 - *Memoirs of Robert E. Lee*
9 - *The Life of Robert E. Lee*, General A.L. Long 1887 J.M. Stoddard & Co. pg. 29
10 - *The Life of Robert E. Lee*, General A.L. Long 1887 J.M. Stoddard & Co. pg. 463
11 - *The Life of Robert E. Lee*, General A.L. Long 1887 J.M. Stoddard & Co. pg. 34
12 - *The Life of Robert E. Lee*, General A.L. Long 1887 J.M. Stoddard & Co. pg. 34
13 - *The Life of Robert E. Lee*, General A.L. Long 1887 J.M. Stoddard & Co. pg. 397
14 - *Anecdotes and Letters of General Robert E. Lee*, Dr. J. William Jones, 1875, D. Appleton & Co., pg. 382
15 - *Biography of Robert E. Lee*, William J. Johnson, Christian Liberty Press
16 - *Recollections and Letters of General Robert E. Lee by his Son*, Doubleday and Page, 1904, pg. 23
17 - *Joy in the Camp: A Brief History of the Spiritual Revival in the Confederate Army* by Charles A. Jennings, Truth in History Publications
18 - *The Life of Robert E. Lee*, General A.L. Long 1887 J.M. Stoddard & Co. pg. 317-318
19 - *Biography of Robert E. Lee*, William J. Johnson, Christian Liberty Press
20 - *Joy in the Camp: A Brief History of the Spiritual Revival in the Confederate Army* by Charles A. Jennings, Truth in History Publications
21 - General Long's personal notebook

22 - *Recollections and Letters of General Robert E. Lee by his Son*, Doubleday and Page, 1904, pg. 172
23 - *Biography of Robert E. Lee*, William J. Johnson, Christian Liberty Press
24 - *Anecdotes and Letters of General Robert E. Lee*, Dr. J. William Jones, 1875, D. Appleton & Co., pg. 113
25 - *The Life of Robert E. Lee*, General A.L. Long 1887 J.M. Stoddard & Co. pg. 451
26 - *Anecdotes and Letters of General Robert E. Lee*, Dr. J. William Jones, 1875, D. Appleton & Co., pg. 113
27 - *Christ in the Camp*, J. William Jones, B. F. Johnson & Co., 1897, pg. 50
28 - *Christ in the Camp*, J. William Jones, B. F. Johnson & Co., 1897, pg. 65
29 - *Christ in the Camp*, J. William Jones, B. F. Johnson & Co., 1897, pg. 65
30 - *Recollections and Letters of General Robert E. Lee by his Son*, Doubleday and Page, 1904, pg. 435
31 - *Robert E. Lee and the Southern Confederacy*, Henry Alexander White, Washington and Lee University, 1911 pg. 437
32 - *Anecdotes and Letters of General Robert E. Lee*, Dr. J. William Jones, 1875, D. Appleton & Co., pg. 177
33 - *The Life of Robert E. Lee*, General A.L. Long 1887 J.M. Stoddard & Co. pg. 447
34 - *Memoirs of Robert E. Lee,* pg. 451
35 - *Biography of Robert E. Lee*, William J. Johnson, Christian Liberty Press
36 - *Biography of Robert E. Lee*, William J. Johnson, Christian Liberty Press
37 - *Lee the College President*, Prof. Edward S. Joynes, University of South Carolina, 1907
38 - *Memorial Discourses*, First Presbyterian Church, Nashville, Tennessee, pg. 11
39 - *Christ in the Camp*, J. William Jones, B. F. Johnson & Co., 1897, pg. 77
40 - *Lee the American*, Gamaliel Bradford, Houghton, Mifflin, Co., 1912, pg. 117
41 - *Lee the American*, Gamaliel Bradford, Houghton, Mifflin, Co., 1912, pg. 242
42 - *Christ in the Camp*, J. William Jones, B. F. Johnson & Co., 1897, pg. 51
43 - *Joy in the Camp: A Brief History of the Spiritual Revival in the Confederate Army* by Charles A. Jennings, Truth in History Publications

44 - *Christ in the Camp*, J. William Jones, B. F. Johnson & Co., 1897, pg. 150
45 - *Anecdotes and Letters of General Robert E. Lee*, Dr. J. William Jones, 1875, D. Appleton & Co., pg. 323
46 - *Memorial Discourses*, First Presbyterian Church, Nashville, Tennessee
47 - *The Chautauquan*, Vol. XXXI, 1900, pg. 189
48 - *Recollections and Letters of General Robert E. Lee by his Son*, Doubleday and Page, 1904, pg. 30
49 - *After Appomattox*, Franklin L. Riley, The Macmillan Co., 1922, pg. 177
50 - *Joy in the Camp: A Brief History of the Spiritual Revival in the Confederate Army* by Charles A. Jennings, Truth in History Publications
51 - *After Appomattox*, Franklin L. Riley, The Macmillan Co., 1922, pg. 177
52 - *Biography of Robert E. Lee*, William J. Johnson, Christian Liberty Press
53 - *The Life of Robert E. Lee*, General A.L. Long 1887 J.M. Stoddard & Co. pg. 365
54 - *The Life of Robert E. Lee*, General A.L. Long 1887 J.M. Stoddard & Co. pg. 366
55 - *The Soul of Lee*, Randolph H. McKim, Longmans, Greene, & Co., 1918, pg. 217
56 - *Marse Robert, Knight of the Confederacy*, James C. Young, Rae D. Henckle, Inc., 1929, pg. 344
57 - *Anecdotes and Letters of General Robert E. Lee*, Dr. J. William Jones, 1875, D. Appleton & Co., pg. 114
58 - *The Need for True Gentleman* by H. Rondel Rumburg, page 3
59 - *Biography of Robert E. Lee*, William J. Johnson, Christian Liberty Press
60 - *Biography of Robert E. Lee*, William J. Johnson, Christian Liberty Press
61 - *Memoirs of Robert E. Lee*
62 - *The Life of Robert E. Lee*, General A.L. Long 1887 J.M. Stoddard & Co. pg. 463
63 - *The Life of Robert E. Lee*, General A.L. Long 1887 J.M. Stoddard & Co. pg. 35
64 - *The Life of Robert E. Lee*, General A.L. Long 1887 J.M. Stoddard & Co. pg. 451
65 - *Anecdotes and Letters of General Robert E. Lee*, Dr. J. William Jones, 1875, D. Appleton & Co., pg. 163
66 - *After Appomattox*, Franklin L. Riley, The Macmillan Co., 1922, pg. 78
67 - *Christ in the Camp*, J. William Jones, B. F. Johnson & Co., 1897, pg. 59

68 - *Anecdotes and Letters of General Robert E. Lee*, Dr. J. William Jones, 1875, D. Appleton & Co., pg. 190
69 - *Recollections and Letters of General Robert E. Lee by his Son*, Doubleday and Page, 1904, pg. 6
70 - *The Life of Robert E. Lee*, General A.L. Long 1887 J.M. Stoddard & Co. pg. 435
71 - *Anecdotes and Letters of General Robert E. Lee*, Dr. J. William Jones, 1875, D. Appleton & Co., pg. 196
72 - *Anecdotes and Letters of General Robert E. Lee*, Dr. J. William Jones, 1875, D. Appleton & Co., pg. 174
73 - *The Soul of Lee*, Randolph H. McKim, Longmans, Greene, & Co., 1918, pg. 190
74 - *Anecdotes and Letters of General Robert E. Lee*, Dr. J. William Jones, 1875, D. Appleton & Co., pg. 187
75 - *Anecdotes and Letters of General Robert E. Lee*, Dr. J. William Jones, 1875, D. Appleton & Co., pg. 195
76 - *Anecdotes and Letters of General Robert E. Lee*, Dr. J. William Jones, 1875, D. Appleton & Co., pg. 196
77 - *Lee the American*, Gamaliel Bradford, Houghton, Mifflin, Co., 1912, pg. 121
78 - *The Life of Robert E. Lee*, General A.L. Long 1887 J.M. Stoddard & Co. pg. 442
79 - *The Life of Robert E. Lee*, General A.L. Long 1887 J.M. Stoddard & Co. pg. 387
80 - *The Life of Robert E. Lee*, General A.L. Long 1887 J.M. Stoddard & Co. pg. 397
81 - *Robert E. Lee*, Philip Alexander Bruce, W. B. Jacobs & Co., 1907, pg. 359
82 - *The Life of Robert E. Lee*, General A.L. Long 1887 J.M. Stoddard & Co. pg. 435
83 - *The Life of Robert E. Lee*, General A.L. Long 1887 J.M. Stoddard & Co. pg. 435
84 - *The Life of Robert E. Lee*, General A.L. Long 1887 J.M. Stoddard & Co. pg. 422
85 - *The Life of Robert E. Lee*, General A.L. Long 1887 J.M. Stoddard & Co. pg. 435
86 - *Memorial Discourses*, First Presbyterian Church, Nashville, Tennessee
87 - *Anecdotes and Letters of General Robert E. Lee*, Dr. J. William Jones, 1875, D. Appleton & Co., pg. 165
88 - *The Life of Robert E. Lee*, General A.L. Long 1887 J.M. Stoddard & Co. pg. 309-310
89 - *The Life of Robert E. Lee*, General A.L. Long 1887 J.M. Stoddard & Co. pg. 433
90 - *The Life of Robert E. Lee*, General A.L. Long 1887 J.M. Stoddard & Co. pg. 433

91 - *The Life of Robert E. Lee*, General A.L. Long 1887 J.M. Stoddard & Co. pg. 31
92 - *The Life and Letters of General Robert E. Lee*, J. William Jones, Neale Publishing Co., pg. 135
93 - *Biography of Robert E. Lee*, William J. Johnson, Christian Liberty Press
94 - *General Lee*, Viscount Wolseley, George P. Humphrey Co., 1906, pg. 5
95 - *The Life of Robert E. Lee*, General A.L. Long 1887 J.M. Stoddard & Co. pg. 417
96 - *The Life of Robert E. Lee*, General A.L. Long 1887 J.M. Stoddard & Co. pg. 435
97 - *The Life of Robert E. Lee*, General A.L. Long 1887 J.M. Stoddard & Co. pg. 433
98 - *The Life of Robert E. Lee*, General A.L. Long 1887 J.M. Stoddard & Co. pg.454
99 - *Recollections and Letters of General Robert E. Lee by his Son*, Doubleday and Page, 1904, pg. 279
100 - *The Life of Robert E. Lee*, General A.L. Long 1887 J.M. Stoddard & Co. pg.417
101 - *Anecdotes and Letters of General Robert E. Lee*, Dr. J. William Jones, 1875, D. Appleton & Co., pg. 174
102 - *The Soul of Lee*, Randolph H. McKim, Longmans, Greene, & Co., 1918, pg. 26
103 - *The Soul of Lee*, Randolph H. McKim, Longmans, Greene, & Co., 1918, pg. 26
104 - *Colonial Churches*, W. M. Clarke, 1907, pg. 138
105 - *Biography of Robert E. Lee*, William J. Johnson, Christian Liberty Press
106 - *The Life of Robert E. Lee*, General A.L. Long 1887 J.M. Stoddard & Co. pg.479
107 - *A Character Sketch of Robert E. Lee* by Charles A. Jennings, Truth in History Publications
108 - *A Character Sketch of Robert E. Lee* by Charles A. Jennings, Truth in History Publications
109 - *Biography of Robert E. Lee*, William J. Johnson, Christian Liberty Press
110 - *Marse Robert, Knight of the Confederacy*, James C. Young, Rae D. Henckle, Inc., 1929, pg. 343
111 - *The Life of Robert E. Lee*, General A.L. Long 1887 J.M. Stoddard & Co. pg.44
112 - *Anecdotes and Letters of General Robert E. Lee*, Dr. J. William Jones, 1875, D. Appleton & Co., pg. 464
113 - *Anecdotes and Letters of General Robert E. Lee*, Dr. J. William Jones, 1875, D. Appleton & Co., pg. 417
114 - *After Appomattox*, Franklin L. Riley, The Macmillan Co.,

1922, pg. 11
115 - *The Life of Robert E. Lee*, General A.L. Long 1887 J.M. Stoddard & Co. pg. 474-475
116 - *Biography of Robert E. Lee*, William J. Johnson, Christian Liberty Press
117 - *Biography of Robert E. Lee*, William J. Johnson, Christian Liberty Press
118 - *Recollections and Letters of General Robert E. Lee by his Son*, Doubleday and Page, 1904, pg. 475
119 - *Anecdotes and Letters of General Robert E. Lee*, Dr. J. William Jones, 1875, D. Appleton & Co., pg. 63
120 - *Anecdotes and Letters of General Robert E. Lee*, Dr. J. William Jones, 1875, D. Appleton & Co., pg. 61
121 - *Anecdotes and Letters of General Robert E. Lee*, Dr. J. William Jones, 1875, D. Appleton & Co., pg. 418
122 - *The Life of Robert E. Lee*, General A.L. Long 1887 J.M. Stoddard & Co. pg. 478-479
123 - *The Life of Robert E. Lee*, General A.L. Long 1887 J.M. Stoddard & Co. pg.479
124 - *The Life of Robert E. Lee*, General A.L. Long 1887 J.M. Stoddard & Co. pg.436
125 - *The Life of Robert E. Lee*, General A.L. Long 1887 J.M. Stoddard & Co. pg.491
126 - *Biography of Robert E. Lee*, William J. Johnson, Christian Liberty Press
127 - http://kudzumedia.com/SouthernPartisan.htm
128 - http://kudzumedia.com/SouthernPartisan.htm
129 - *The 21 Irrefutable Laws of Leadership* – John C. Maxwell, cINJOY, Inc.
130 *The Need for True Gentleman* by H. Rondel Rumburg, pg. 1
131 - *Popular Life of General Robert E. Lee*, Emily V. Mason, 1874, J. Murphy & Company, pg. 21
132 - *Biography of Robert E. Lee*, William J. Johnson, Christian Liberty Press
133 - Article by a Mrs. Pickett in *Lippincott's Magzine*, Volume 79, pg. 52
134 - *Biography of Robert E. Lee*, William J. Johnson, Christian Liberty Press
135 - *Personal Reminiscences, Anecdotes, and Letters of General Robert E. Lee*, Dr. J. William Jones, 1875, D. Appleton & Co., pg. 138
136 - *Lee the American*, Gamaliel Bradford, Houghton, Mifflin, Co., 1912, pg. 28
137 - *Recollections and Letters of General Robert E. Lee by his Son*, Doubleday and Page, 1904, pg. 24

138 - *Robert E. Lee, The Southerner*, Thomas Nelson Page, Charles Scribner & Sons, 1908, pg. 54)
139 - *The Life of Robert E. Lee*, General A.L. Long 1887 J.M. Stoddard & Co., pg. 102
140 - *The Life of Robert E. Lee*, General A.L. Long 1887 J.M. Stoddard & Co., pg. 392
141- *The Life of Robert E. Lee*, General A.L. Long 1887 J.M. Stoddard & Co., pg 400 – 401
142 - *The Life of Robert E. Lee*, General A.L. Long 1887 J.M. Stoddard & Co., pg. 61)
143 - *The Life of Robert E. Lee*, General A.L. Long 1887 J.M. Stoddard & Co., pg. 92)
144 - *The Life of Robert E. Lee*, General A.L. Long 1887 J.M. Stoddard & Co., pg. 482)
145 - *Memoirs of Robert E. Lee*, pg. 73
146 - *The Life of Robert E. Lee*, General A.L. Long 1887 J.M. Stoddard & Co., pg. 426
147 - *Personal Reminiscences, Anecdotes, and Letters of General Robert E. Lee*, Dr. J. William Jones, 1875, D. Appleton & Co., pg. 168)
148 - *The Life of Robert E. Lee*, General A.L. Long 1887 J.M. Stoddard & Co., pg. 427
149 - *Personal Reminiscences, Anecdotes, and Letters of General Robert E. Lee*, Dr. J. William Jones, 1875, D. Appleton & Co., pg. 173)
150 - *Personal Reminiscences, Anecdotes, and Letters of General Robert E. Lee*, Dr. J. William Jones, 1875, D. Appleton & Co., pg. 319
151 - *Personal Reminiscences, Anecdotes, and Letters of General Robert E. Lee*, Dr. J. William Jones, 1875, D. Appleton & Co., pg. 72)
152 - *The Life of Robert E. Lee*, General A.L. Long 1887 J.M. Stoddard & Co., pg. 66
153 - *The Life of Robert E. Lee*, General A.L. Long 1887 J.M. Stoddard & Co., pg. 420
154 - *The Life of Robert E. Lee*, General A.L. Long 1887 J.M. Stoddard & Co., pg. 427
155 - *The Life of Robert E. Lee*, General A.L. Long 1887 J.M. Stoddard & Co., pg. 427
156 - *The Life of Robert E. Lee*, General A.L. Long 1887 J.M. Stoddard & Co., pg 74
157 - *The Soul of Lee*, Randolph H. McKim, Longmans, Greene, & Co., 1918, pg. 189
158 - *Personal Reminiscences, Anecdotes, and Letters of General Robert E. Lee*, Dr. J. William Jones, 1875, D. Appleton & Co., pg. 170

159 - *The Life of Robert E. Lee*, General A.L. Long 1887 J.M. Stoddard & Co., pg 469
160 - *Memoirs of Robert E. Lee*
161 - *Biography of Robert E. Lee*, William J. Johnson, Christian Liberty Press
162 - *The Life of Robert E. Lee*, General A.L. Long 1887 J.M. Stoddard & Co., pg. 397)

ADDITIONAL MATERIALS
Authored by Edward R. DeVries

Prices include domestic postage & handling

A Symbol of Hate? or an Ensign of the Christian Faith?
$10.00

>10 chapters with 61 End Notes. A best-selling book that tells the truth about the Confederate Battle Flag and its Christian origin.

The Truth about the Confederate Battle Flag (video)
$10.00

>A 55-minute video presentation of the material documented in the book A Symbol of Hate? or an Ensign of the Christian Faith?

The Christian Testimony of General Robert E. Lee
$10.00

>An hour-and-a-half video presentation of the material documented in this book. Also features a presentation by the Hon. Judge James Morgan and "southern" music by *Cross Ties*.

The Christian Testimony of Gen. "Stonewall" Jackson
$10.00

>An hour-long video presentation on the life and faith of Thomas J. Jackson. Was "Stonewall" really as religious as he was portrayed to be in the movie Gods and Generals?